STILLNESS
SPEAKS

Also by Eckhart Tolle

The Power of Now

Practicing the Power of Now

STILLNESS SPEAKS

ECKHART TOLLE

YogiImpressions®

YogiImpressions®

Yogi Impressions LLP
1711, Centre 1, World Trade Centre,
Cuffe Parade, Mumbai 400 005, India.
Website: www.yogiimpressions.com

Cover design by Mary Ann Casler
Text design and typography by Tona Pearce Myers
Author photo by Rick Tang
Cover image from Desert Dolphin

Originally published in the United States by
New World Library, 2003

First India printing: August 2003
Sixteenth reprint: February 2018
ISBN 978-81-88479-46-7

Printed at: Repro India Ltd., Mumbai

CONTENTS

FOREWORD

Albert Einstein said, "Stand still. The trees ahead and bush beside you are not lost."

In this age when our minds are running to nowhere on treadmills — and getting there fast — Eckhart's message in *Stillness Speaks* is loud and clear.

— Gautam Sachdeva

INTRODUCTION

A true spiritual teacher does not have anything to teach in the conventional sense of the word, does not have anything to give or add to you, such as new information, beliefs, or rules of conduct. The only function of such a teacher is to help you remove that which separates you from the truth of who you already are and what you already know in the depth of your being. The spiritual teacher is there to uncover and reveal to you that dimension of inner depth that is also peace.

If you come to a spiritual teacher — or this book — looking for stimulating ideas, theories, beliefs, intellectual discussions, then you will be disappointed. In other words, if you are looking for food for thought, you won't find it, and you will miss the very essence of the teaching, the essence of this book, which is not in the words but within yourself. It is good to remember that, to feel that, as you read. The words are no more than signposts. That to which they point is not to be found within the realm of thought, but a dimension within yourself that is deeper and infinitely vaster than thought. A vibrantly alive peace is one of the characteristics of that dimension, so whenever you feel inner peace arising as you read, the book is doing its work and fulfilling its function as your teacher: it is reminding you of who you are and pointing the way back home.

This is not a book to be read from cover to cover and then put away. Live with it, pick it up frequently, and, more importantly, put it down frequently, or spend more time holding it than reading it. Many readers will feel naturally inclined to stop reading after each entry, to pause, reflect, become still. It is always more helpful and more important to stop reading than to continue reading. Allow the book to do its work, to awaken you from the old grooves of your repetitive and conditioned thinking.

The form of this book can be seen as a revival for the present age of the oldest form of recorded spiritual teachings: the sutras of ancient India. Sutras are powerful pointers to the truth in the form of aphorisms or short sayings, with little conceptual elaboration. The Vedas and Upanishads are the early sacred teachings recorded in the form of sutras, as are the words of the Buddha. The sayings and parables of Jesus, too, when taken out of their narrative context, could be regarded as sutras, as well as the profound teachings contained in the *Tao Te Ching*, the ancient Chinese book of wisdom. The advantage of the sutra form lies in its brevity. It does not engage the thinking mind more than is necessary. What it doesn't say — but only points to — is more important than what it says. The sutra-like character of the writings in this book is particularly marked in chapter 1 ("Silence & Stillness"), which contains only the briefest of entries. This chapter contains the essence of the entire book and may be all that some readers require. The other chapters are there for those who need a few more signposts.

Just like the ancient sutras, the writings contained within this book are sacred and have come out of a state of consciousness we may call stillness. Unlike those ancient sutras, however, they don't belong to any one religion or spiritual tradition, but are immediately accessible to the whole of humanity. There is also an added sense of urgency here. The transformation of human consciousness is no longer a luxury, so to speak, available only to a few isolated individuals, but a necessity if humankind is not to destroy itself. At the present time, the dysfunction of the old consciousness and the arising of the new are both accelerating. Paradoxically, things are getting worse and better at the same time, although the worse is more apparent because it makes so much "noise."

This book, of course, uses words that in the act of reading become thoughts in your mind. But those are not ordinary thoughts — repetitive, noisy, self-serving, clamoring for attention. Just like every true spiritual teacher, just like the ancient sutras, the thoughts within this book don't say, "Look at me," but "Look beyond me." Because the thoughts came out of stillness, they have power — the power to take you back into the same stillness from which they arose. That stillness is also inner peace, and that stillness and peace are the essence of your Being. It is inner stillness that will save and transform the world.

CHAPTER I

~

SILENCE & STILLNESS

When you lose touch with inner stillness, you lose touch with yourself. When you lose touch with yourself, you lose yourself in the world.

Your innermost sense of self, of who you are, is inseparable from stillness. This is the *I Am* that is deeper than name and form.

Stillness is your essential nature. What is stillness? The inner space or awareness in which the words on this page are being perceived and become thoughts. Without that awareness, there would be no perception, no thoughts, no world.

You are that awareness, disguised as a person.

The equivalent of external noise is the inner noise of thinking. The equivalent of external silence is inner stillness.

Whenever there is some silence around you — listen to it. That means just notice it. Pay attention to it. Listening to silence awakens the dimension of stillness within yourself, because it is only through stillness that you can be aware of silence.

See that in the moment of noticing the silence around you, you are not thinking. You are aware, but not thinking.

When you become aware of silence, immediately there is that state of inner still alertness. You are present. You have stepped out of thousands of years of collective human conditioning.

Look at a tree, a flower, a plant. Let your awareness rest upon it. How still they are, how deeply rooted in Being. Allow nature to teach you stillness.

When you look at a tree and perceive its stillness, you become still yourself. You connect with it at a very deep level. You feel a oneness with whatever you perceive in and through stillness. Feeling the oneness of yourself with all things is true love.

Silence is helpful, but you don't need it in order to find stillness. Even when there is noise, you can be aware of the stillness underneath the noise, of the space in which the noise arises. That is the inner space of pure awareness, consciousness itself.

You can become aware of awareness as the background to all your sense perceptions, all your thinking. Becoming aware of awareness is the arising of inner stillness.

Any disturbing noise can be as helpful as silence. How? By dropping your inner resistance to the noise, by allowing it to be as it is, this acceptance also takes you into that realm of inner peace that is stillness.

Whenever you deeply accept this moment as it is — no matter what form it takes — you are still, you are at peace.

Pay attention to the gap — the gap between two thoughts, the brief, silent space between words in a conversation, between the notes of a piano or flute, or the gap between the in-breath and out-breath.

When you pay attention to those gaps, awareness of "something" becomes — just awareness. The formless dimension of pure consciousness arises from within you and replaces identification with form.

True intelligence operates silently. Stillness is where creativity and solutions to problems are found.

Is stillness just the absence of noise and content? No, it is intelligence itself — the underlying consciousness out of which every form is born. And how could that be separate from who you are?

The form that you think you are came out of that and is being sustained by it.

It is the essence of all galaxies and blades of grass; of all flowers, trees, birds, and all other forms.

Stillness is the only thing in this world that has no form. But then, it is not really a thing, and it is not of this world.

When you look at a tree or a human being in stillness, who is looking? Something deeper than the person. Consciousness is looking at its creation.

In the Bible, it says that God created the world and saw that it was good. That is what you see when you look from stillness without thought.

Do you need more knowledge? Is more information going to save the world, or faster computers, more scientific or intellectual analysis? Is it not wisdom that humanity needs most at this time?

But what is wisdom and where is it to be found? Wisdom comes with the ability to be still. Just look and just listen. No more is needed. Being still, looking, and listening activates the non-conceptual intelligence within you. Let stillness direct your words and actions.

CHAPTER 2

BEYOND THE THINKING MIND

The human condition: lost in thought.

Most people spend their entire life imprisoned within the confines of their own thoughts. They never go beyond a narrow, mind-made, personalized sense of self that is conditioned by the past.

In you, as in each human being, there is a dimension of consciousness far deeper than thought. It is the very essence of who you are. We may call it presence, awareness, the unconditioned consciousness. In the ancient teachings, it is the Christ within, or your Buddha nature.

Finding that dimension frees you and the world from the suffering you inflict on yourself and others when the mind-made "little me" is all you know and runs your life. Love, joy, creative expansion, and lasting inner peace cannot come into your life except through that unconditioned dimension of consciousness.

If you can recognize, even occasionally, the thoughts that go through your mind as simply thoughts, if you can witness your own mental-emotional reactive patterns as they happen, then that dimension is already emerging in you as the awareness in which thoughts and emotions happen — the timeless inner space in which the content of your life unfolds.

The stream of thinking has enormous momentum that can easily drag you along with it. Every thought pretends that it matters so much. It wants to draw your attention in completely.

Here is a new spiritual practice for you: don't take your thoughts too seriously.

How easy it is for people to become trapped in their conceptual prisons.

The human mind, in its desire to know, understand, and control, mistakes its opinions and viewpoints for the truth. It says: this is how it is. You have to be larger than thought to realize that however you interpret "your life" or someone else's life or behavior, however you judge any situation, it is no more than a viewpoint, one of many possible perspectives. It is no more than a bundle of thoughts. But reality is one unified whole, in which all things are interwoven, where nothing exists in and by itself. Thinking fragments reality — it cuts it up into conceptual bits and pieces.

The thinking mind is a useful and powerful tool, but it is also very limiting when it takes over your life completely, when you don't realize that it is only a small aspect of the consciousness that you are.

Wisdom is not a product of thought. The deep *knowing* that is wisdom arises through the simple act of giving someone or something your full attention. Attention is primordial intelligence, consciousness itself. It dissolves the barriers created by conceptual thought, and with this comes the recognition that nothing exists in and by itself. It joins the perceiver and the perceived in a unifying field of awareness. It is the healer of separation.

Whenever you are immersed in compulsive thinking, you are avoiding what is. You don't want to be where you are. Here, Now.

Dogmas — religious, political, scientific — arise out of the erroneous belief that thought can encapsulate reality or the truth. Dogmas are collective conceptual prisons. And the strange thing is that people love their prison cells because they give them a sense of security and a false sense of "I know."

Nothing has inflicted more suffering on humanity than its dogmas. It is true that every dogma crumbles sooner or later, because reality will eventually disclose its falseness; however, unless the basic delusion of it is seen for what it is, it will be replaced by others.

What is this basic delusion? Identification with thought.

Spiritual awakening is awakening from the dream of thought.

The realm of consciousness is much vaster than thought can grasp. When you no longer believe everything you think, you step out of thought and see clearly that the thinker is not who you are.

The mind exists in a state of "not enough" and so is always greedy for more. When you are identified with mind, you get bored and restless very easily. Boredom means the mind is hungry for more stimulus, more food for thought, and its hunger is not being satisfied.

When you feel bored, you can satisfy the mind's hunger by picking up a magazine, making a phone call, switching on the TV, surfing the web, going shopping, or — and this is not uncommon — transferring the mental sense of lack and its need for *more* to the body and satisfy it briefly by ingesting more food.

Or you can stay bored and restless and observe what it feels like to be bored and restless. As you bring awareness to the feeling, there is suddenly some space and stillness around it, as it were. A little at first, but as the sense of inner space grows, the feeling of boredom will begin to diminish in intensity and significance. So even boredom can teach you who you are and who you are not.

You discover that a "bored person" is not who you are. Boredom is simply a conditioned energy movement within you. Neither are you an angry, sad, or fearful person. Boredom, anger, sadness, or fear are not "yours," not personal. They are conditions of the human mind. They come and go.

Nothing that comes and goes is you.

"I am bored." Who knows this?

"I am angry, sad, afraid." Who knows this?

You are the knowing, not the condition that is known.

Prejudice of any kind implies that you are identified with the thinking mind. It means you don't see the other human being anymore, but only your own concept of that human being. To reduce the aliveness of another human being to a concept is already a form of violence.

Thinking that is not rooted in awareness becomes self-serving and dysfunctional. Cleverness devoid of wisdom is extremely dangerous and destructive. That is the current state of most of humanity. The amplification of thought as science and technology, although intrinsically neither good nor bad, has also become destructive because so often the thinking out of which it comes has no roots in awareness.

The next step in human evolution is to transcend thought. This is now our urgent task. It doesn't mean not to think anymore, but simply not to be completely identified with thought, possessed by thought.

Feel the energy of your inner body. Immediately mental noise slows down or ceases. Feel it in your hands, your feet, your abdomen, your chest. Feel the life that you are, the life that animates the body.

The body then becomes a doorway, so to speak, into a deeper sense of aliveness underneath the fluctuating emotions and underneath your thinking.

There is an aliveness in you that you can feel with your entire Being, not just in the head. Every cell is alive in that presence in which you don't need to think. Yet, in that state, if thought is required for some practical purpose, it is there. The mind can still operate, and it operates beautifully when the greater intelligence that you *are* uses it and expresses itself through it.

You may have overlooked that brief periods in which you are "conscious without thought" are already occurring naturally and spontaneously in your life. You may be engaged in some manual activity, or walking across the room, or waiting at the airline counter, and be so completely present that the usual mental static of thought subsides and is replaced by an aware presence. Or you may find yourself looking at the sky or listening to someone without any inner mental commentary. Your perceptions become crystal clear, unclouded by thought.

To the mind, all this is not significant, because it has "more important" things to think about. It is also not memorable, and that's why you may have overlooked that it is already happening.

The truth is that it is the most significant thing that *can* happen to you. It is the beginning of a shift from thinking to aware presence.

Become at ease with the state of "not knowing." This takes you beyond mind because the mind is always trying to conclude and interpret. It is afraid of not knowing. So, when you can be at ease with not knowing, you have already gone beyond the mind. A deeper knowing that is non-conceptual then arises out of that state.

Artistic creation, sports, dance, teaching, counseling — mastery in any field of endeavor implies that the thinking mind is either no longer involved at all or at least is taking second place. A power and intelligence greater than you and yet one with you in essence takes over. There is no decision-making process anymore; spontaneous right action happens, and "you" are not doing it. Mastery of life is the opposite of control. You become aligned with the greater consciousness. *It* acts, speaks, does the works.

A moment of danger can bring about a temporary cessation of the stream of thinking and thus give you a taste of what it means to be present, alert, aware.

The Truth is far more all-encompassing than the mind could ever comprehend. No thought can encapsulate the Truth. At best, it can point to it. For example, it can say: "All things are intrinsically one." That is a pointer, not an explanation. Understanding these words means *feeling* deep within you the truth to which they point.

CHAPTER 3

~

THE EGOIC SELF

The mind is incessantly looking not only for food for thought; it is looking for food for its identity, its sense of self. This is how the ego comes into existence and continuously re-creates itself.

When you think or speak about yourself, when you say, "I," what you usually refer to is "me and my story." This is the "I" of your likes and dislikes, fears and desires, the "I" that is never satisfied for long. It is a mind-made sense of who you are, conditioned by the past and seeking to find its fulfillment in the future.

Can you see that this "I" is fleeting, a temporary formation, like a wave pattern on the surface of the water?

Who is it that sees this? Who is it that is *aware* of the fleetingness of your physical and psychological form? I Am. This is the deeper "I" that has nothing to do with past and future.

What will be left of all the fearing and wanting associated with your problematic life situation that every day takes up most of your attention? A dash — one or two inches long, between the date of birth and date of death on your gravestone.

To the egoic self, this is a depressing thought. To you, it is liberating.

When each thought absorbs your attention completely, it means you identify with the voice in your head. Thought then becomes invested with a sense of self. This is the ego, a mind-made "me." That mentally constructed self feels incomplete and precarious. That's why fearing and wanting are its predominant emotions and motivating forces.

When you recognize that there is a voice in your head that pretends to be you and never stops speaking, you are awakening out of your unconscious identification with the stream of thinking. When you notice that voice, you realize that who you are is not the voice — the thinker — but the one who is aware of it.

Knowing yourself as the awareness behind the voice is freedom.

The egoic self is always engaged in seeking. It is seeking more of this or that to add to itself, to make itself feel more complete. This explains the ego's compulsive preoccupation with future.

Whenever you become aware of yourself "living for the next moment," you have already stepped out of that egoic mind pattern, and the possibility of choosing to give your full attention to this moment arises simultaneously.

By giving your full attention to this moment, an intelligence far greater than the egoic mind enters your life.

When you live through the ego, you always reduce the present moment to a means to an end. You live for the future, and when you achieve your goals, they don't satisfy you, at least not for long.

When you give more attention to the doing than to the future result that you want to achieve through it, you break the old egoic conditioning. Your doing then becomes not only a great deal more effective, but infinitely more fulfilling and joyful.

Almost every ego contains at least an element of what we might call "victim identity." Some people have such a strong victim image of themselves that it becomes the central core of their ego. Resentment and grievances form an essential part of their sense of self.

Even if your grievances are completely "justified," you have constructed an identity for yourself that is much like a prison whose bars are made of thought forms. See what you are doing to yourself, or rather what your mind is doing to you. Feel the emotional attachment you have to your victim story and become aware of the compulsion to think or talk about it. Be there as the witnessing presence of your inner state. You don't have to *do* anything. With awareness comes transformation and freedom.

Complaining and reactivity are favorite mind patterns through which the ego strengthens itself. For many people, a large part of their mental-emotional activity consists of complaining and reacting against this or that. By doing this, you make others or a situation "wrong" and yourself "right." Through being "right," you feel superior, and through feeling superior, you strengthen your sense of self. In reality, of course, you are only strengthening the illusion of ego.

Can you observe those patterns within yourself and recognize the complaining voice in your head for what it is?

The egoic sense of self needs conflict because its sense of a separate identity gets strengthened in fighting against this or that, and in demonstrating that this is "me" and that is not "me."

Not infrequently, tribes, nations, and religions derive a strengthened sense of collective identity from having enemies. Who would the "believer" be without the "unbeliever"?

In your dealings with people, can you detect subtle feelings of either superiority or inferiority toward them? You are looking at the ego, which lives through comparison.

Envy is a by-product of the ego, which feels diminished if something good happens to someone else, or someone has more, knows more, or can do more than you. The ego's identity depends on comparison and feeds on *more*. It will grasp at anything. If all else fails, you can strengthen your fictitious sense of self through seeing yourself as *more* unfairly treated by life or *more* ill than someone else.

What are the stories, the fictions from which you derive your sense of self?

Built into the very structure of the egoic self is a need to oppose, resist, and exclude to maintain the sense of separateness on which its continued survival depends. So there is "me" against the "other," "us" against "them."

The ego needs to be in conflict with something or someone. That explains why you are looking for peace and joy and love but cannot tolerate them for very long. You say you want happiness but are addicted to your unhappiness.

Your unhappiness ultimately arises not from the circumstances of your life but from the conditioning of your mind.

Do you carry feelings of guilt about something you did — or failed to do — in the past? This much is certain: you acted according to your level of consciousness or rather unconsciousness at that time. If you had been more aware, more conscious, you would have acted differently.

Guilt is another attempt by the ego to create an identity, a sense of self. To the ego, it doesn't matter whether that self is positive or negative. What you did or failed to do was a manifestation of unconsciousness — human unconsciousness. The ego, however, personalizes it and says, "I did that," and so you carry a mental image of yourself as "bad."

Throughout history humans have inflicted countless violent, cruel, and hurtful acts on each other, and continue to do so. Are they all to be condemned; are they all guilty? Or are those acts simply expressions of unconsciousness, an evolutionary stage that we are now growing out of?

Jesus' words, "Forgive them for they know not what they do," also apply to yourself.

If you set egoic goals for the purpose of freeing yourself, enhancing yourself or your sense of importance, even if you achieve them, they will not satisfy you.

Set goals, but know that the arriving is not all that important. When anything arises out of presence, it means this moment is not a means to an end: the doing is fulfilling in itself every moment. You are no longer reducing the Now to a means to an end, which is the egoic consciousness.

~

"No self. No problem," said the Buddhist Master when asked to explain the deeper meaning of Buddhism.

~

CHAPTER 4

~

THE NOW

On the surface it seems that the present moment is only one of many, many moments. Each day of your life appears to consist of thousands of moments where different things happen. Yet if you look more deeply, is there not only one moment, ever? Is life ever not "this moment"?

This one moment — Now — is the only thing you can never escape from, the one constant factor in your life. No matter what happens, no matter how much your life changes, one thing is certain: it's always Now.

Since there is no escape from the Now, why not welcome it, become friendly with it?

When you make friends with the present moment, you feel at home no matter where you are. When you don't feel at home in the Now, no matter where you go, you will carry unease with you.

The present moment is as it is. Always. Can you let it be?

The division of life into past, present, and future is mind-made and ultimately illusory. Past and future are thought forms, mental abstractions. The past can only be remembered Now. What you remember is an event that took place in the Now, and you remember it Now. The future, when it comes, is the Now. So the only thing that is real, the only thing there ever is *is* the Now.

To have your attention in the Now is not a denial of what is needed in your life. It is recognizing what is primary. Then you can deal with what is secondary with great ease. It is not saying, "I'm not dealing with things anymore because there is only the Now." No. Find what is primary first, and make the Now into your friend, not your enemy. Acknowledge it, honor it. When the Now is the foundation and primary focus of your life, then your life unfolds with ease.

Putting away the dishes, drawing up a business strategy, planning a trip — what is more important: the doing or the result that you want to achieve through the doing? This moment or some future moment?

Do you treat *this moment* as if it were an obstacle to be overcome? Do you feel you have a future moment to get to that is more important?

Almost everyone lives like this most of the time. Since the future never arrives, except *as* the present, it is a dysfunctional way to live. It generates a constant undercurrent of unease, tension, and discontent. It does not honor life, which is Now and never not Now.

Feel the aliveness within your body. That anchors you in the Now.

Ultimately you are not taking responsibility for life until you take responsibility for *this moment* — Now. This is because Now is the only place where life can be found.

Taking responsibility for this moment means not to oppose internally the "suchness" of Now, not to argue with what is. It means to be in alignment with life.

The Now is as it is because it cannot be otherwise. What Buddhists have always known, physicists now confirm: there are no isolated things or events. Underneath the surface appearance, all things are interconnected, are part of the totality of the cosmos that has brought about the form that this moment takes.

When you say "yes" to what is, you become aligned with the power and intelligence of Life itself. Only then can you become an agent for positive change in the world.

A simple but radical spiritual practice is to accept whatever arises in the Now — within and without.

When your attention moves into the Now, there is an alertness. It is as if you were waking up from a dream, the dream of thought, the dream of past and future. Such clarity, such simplicity. No room for problem-making. Just this moment as it is.

The moment you enter the Now with your attention, you realize that life is sacred. There is a sacredness to everything you perceive when you are present. The more you live in the Now, the more you sense the simple yet profound joy of Being and the sacredness of all life.

Most people confuse the Now with *what happens* in the Now, but that's not what it is. The Now is deeper than what happens in it. It is the space in which it happens.

So do not confuse the content of this moment with the Now. The Now is deeper than any content that arises in it.

When you step into the Now, you step out of the content of your mind. The incessant stream of thinking slows down. Thoughts don't absorb all your attention anymore, don't draw you in totally. Gaps arise in between thoughts — spaciousness, stillness. You begin to realize how much vaster and deeper you are than your thoughts.

Thoughts, emotions, sense perceptions, and whatever you experience make up the content of your life. "My life" is what you derive your sense of self from, and "my life" is content, or so you believe.

You continuously overlook the most obvious fact: your innermost sense of *I Am* has nothing to do with what *happens* in your life, nothing to do with content. That sense of *I Am* is one with the Now. It always remains the same. In childhood and old age, in health or sickness, in success or failure, the *I Am* — the space of Now — remains unchanged at its deepest level. It usually gets confused with content, and so you experience *I Am* or the Now only faintly and indirectly, *through* the content of your life. In other words: your sense of Being becomes obscured by circumstances, your stream of thinking, and the many things of this world. The Now becomes obscured by time.

And so you forget your rootedness in Being, your divine reality, and lose yourself in the world. Confusion, anger, depression, violence, and conflict arise when humans forget who they are.

Yet how easy it is to remember the truth and thus return home:

I am not my thoughts, emotions, sense perceptions, and experiences. I am not the content of
my life. I am Life. I am the space in which all
things happen. I am consciousness. I am the Now.
I Am.

CHAPTER 5

~

WHO YOU TRULY ARE

The Now is inseparable from who you are at the deepest level.

~

Many things in your life matter, but only one thing matters absolutely.

It matters whether you succeed or fail in the eyes of the world. It matters whether you are healthy or not healthy, whether you are educated or not educated. It matters whether you are rich or poor — it certainly makes a difference in your life. Yes, all these things matter, relatively speaking, but they don't matter absolutely.

There is something that matters more than any of those things and that is finding the essence of who you are beyond that short-lived entity, that short-lived personalized sense of self.

You find peace not by rearranging the circumstances of your life, but by realizing who you are at the deepest level.

∼

Reincarnation doesn't help you if in your next incarnation you still don't know who you are.

∼

All the misery on the planet arises due to a personalized sense of "me" or "us." That covers up the essence of who you are. When you are unaware of that inner essence, in the end you always create misery. It's as simple as that. When you don't know who you are, you create a mind-made self as a substitute for your beautiful divine being and cling to that fearful and needy self.

Protecting and enhancing that false sense of self then becomes your primary motivating force.

Many expressions that are in common usage, and sometimes the structure of language itself, reveal the fact that people don't know who they are. You say: "He lost his life" or "my life," as if life were something that you can possess or lose. The truth is: you don't *have* a life, you *are* life. The One Life, the one consciousness that pervades the entire universe and takes temporary form to experience itself as a stone or a blade of grass, as an animal, a person, a star or a galaxy.

Can you sense deep within that you already know that? Can you sense that you already are That?

For most things in life, you need time: to learn a new skill, build a house, become an expert, make a cup of tea.... Time is useless, however, for the most essential thing in life, the one thing that really matters: self-realization, which means knowing who you are beyond the surface self — beyond your name, your physical form, your history, your story.

You cannot find yourself in the past or future. The only place where you can find yourself is in the Now.

Spiritual seekers look for self-realization or enlightenment in the future. To be a seeker implies that you need the future. If this is what you believe, it becomes true for you: you *will* need time until you realize that you don't need time to be who you are.

When you look at a tree, you are aware of the tree. When you have a thought or feeling, you are aware of that thought or feeling. When you have a pleasurable or painful experience, you are aware of that experience.

These seem to be true and obvious statements, yet if you look at them very closely, you will find that in a subtle way their very structure contains a fundamental illusion, an illusion that is unavoidable when you use language. Thought and language create an apparent duality and a separate person where there is none. The truth is: you are not somebody who is aware of the tree, the thought, feeling, or experience. You are the awareness or consciousness in and by which those things appear.

As you go about your life, can you be aware of yourself as the awareness in which the entire content of your life unfolds?

You say, "I want to know myself." You *are* the "I." You *are* the Knowing. You *are* the consciousness through which everything is known. And that cannot *know* itself; it *is* itself.

There is nothing to know beyond that, and yet all knowing arises out of it. The "I" cannot make itself into an object of knowledge, of consciousness.

So you cannot become an object to yourself. That is the very reason the illusion of egoic identity arose — because mentally you made yourself into an object. "That's me," you say. And then you begin to have a relationship with yourself, and tell others and yourself your story.

By knowing yourself as the awareness in which phenomenal existence happens, you become free of dependency on phenomena and free of self-seeking in situations, places, and conditions. In other words: what happens or doesn't happen is not that important anymore. Things lose their heaviness, their seriousness. A playfulness comes into your life. You recognize this world as a cosmic dance, the dance of form — no more and no less.

When you know who you truly are, there is an abiding alive sense of peace. You could call it joy because that's what joy is: vibrantly alive peace. It is the joy of knowing yourself as the very life essence before life takes on form. That is the joy of Being — of being who you truly are.

Just as water can be solid, liquid, or gaseous, consciousness can be seen to be "frozen" as physical matter, "liquid" as mind and thought, or formless as pure consciousness.

Pure consciousness is Life before it comes into manifestation, and that Life looks at the world of form through "your" eyes because consciousness is who you are. When you know yourself as That, then you recognize yourself in everything. It is a state of complete clarity of perception. You are no longer an entity with a heavy past that becomes a screen of concepts through which every experience is interpreted.

When you perceive without interpretation, you can then sense what it is that is perceiving. The most we can say in language is that there is a field of alert stillness in which the perception happens.

Through "you," formless consciousness has become aware of itself.

Most people's lives are run by desire and fear.

Desire is the need to *add* something to yourself in order to *be* yourself more fully. All fear is the fear of *losing* something and thereby becoming diminished and *being* less.

These two movements obscure the fact that Being cannot be given or taken away. Being in its fullness is already within you, Now.

CHAPTER 6

ACCEPTANCE & SURRENDER

Whenever you are able, have a "look" inside yourself to see whether you are unconsciously creating conflict between the inner and the outer, between your external circumstances at that moment — where you are, who you are with, or what you are doing — and your thoughts and feelings. Can you feel how painful it is to internally stand in opposition to what *is?*

When you recognize this, you also realize that you are now free to give up this futile conflict, this inner state of war.

How often each day, if you were to verbalize your inner reality at that moment, would you have to say, "I don't want to be where I am"? What does it feel like when you don't want to be where you are — the traffic jam, your place of work, the airport lounge, the people you are with?

It is true, of course, that some places are good places to walk out of — and sometimes that may well be the most appropriate thing for you to do. In many cases, however, walking out is not an option. In all those cases, the "I don't want to be here" is not only useless but also dysfunctional. It makes you and others unhappy.

It has been said: wherever you go, there you are. In other words: you are here. Always. Is it so hard to accept that?

Do you really need to mentally label every sense perception and experience? Do you really need to have a reactive like/dislike relationship with life where you are in almost continuous conflict with situations and people? Or is that just a deep-seated mental habit that can be broken? Not by doing anything, but by allowing this moment to be as it is.

The habitual and reactive "no" strengthens the ego. "Yes" weakens it. Your form identity, the ego, cannot survive surrender.

"I have so much to do." Yes, but what is the quality of your doing? Driving to work, speaking to clients, working on the computer, running errands, dealing with the countless things that make up your daily life — how total are you in what you do? Is your doing surrendered or non-surrendered? This is what determines your success in life, not how much effort you make. Effort implies stress and strain, *needing* to reach a certain point in the future or accomplish a certain result.

Can you detect even the slightest element within yourself of *not wanting* to be doing what you are doing? That is a denial of life, and so a truly successful outcome is not possible.

If you can detect this within yourself, can you also drop it and be total in what you do?

~

"Doing one thing at a time" is how one Zen Master defined the essence of Zen.

Doing one thing at a time means to be total in what you do, to give it your complete attention. This is surrendered action — empowered action.

~

Your acceptance of what *is* takes you to a deeper level where your inner state as well as your sense of self no longer depend on the mind's judgments of "good" or "bad."

When you say "yes" to the "isness" of life, when you accept this moment as it is, you can feel a sense of spaciousness within you that is deeply peaceful.

On the surface, you may still be happy when it's sunny and not so happy when it's rainy; you may be happy at winning a million dollars and unhappy at losing all your possessions. Neither happiness nor unhappiness, however, go all that deep anymore. They are ripples on the surface of your Being. The background peace within you remains undisturbed regardless of the nature of the outside condition.

The "yes" to what *is* reveals a dimension of depth within you that is dependent neither on external conditions nor on the internal conditions of con-stantly fluctuating thoughts and emotions.

Surrender becomes so much easier when you realize the fleeting nature of all experiences and that the world cannot give you anything of lasting value. You then continue to meet people, to be involved in experiences and activities, but without the wants and fears of the egoic self. That is to say, you no longer demand that a situation, person, place, or event should satisfy you or make you happy. Its passing and imperfect nature is allowed to be.

And the miracle is that when you are no longer placing an impossible demand on it, every situation, person, place, or event becomes not only satisfying but also more harmonious, more peaceful.

When you completely accept this moment, when you no longer argue with what *is,* the compulsion to think lessens and is replaced by an alert stillness. You are fully conscious, yet the mind is not labeling this moment in any way. This state of inner nonresistance opens you to the unconditioned consciousness that is infinitely greater than the human mind. This vast intelligence can then express itself through you and assist you, both from within and from without. That is why, by letting go of inner resistance, you often find circumstances change for the better.

Am I saying, "Enjoy this moment. Be happy"? No.

Allow the "suchness" of this moment. That's enough.

Surrender is surrender to *this moment,* not to a story through which you *interpret* this moment and then try to resign yourself to it.

For instance, you may have a disability and can't walk anymore. The condition is as it is.

Perhaps your mind is now creating a story that says, "This is what my life has come to. I have ended up in a wheelchair. Life has treated me harshly and unfairly. I don't deserve this."

Can you accept the *isness* of this moment and not confuse it with a story the mind has created around it?

Surrender comes when you no longer ask, "Why is this happening to me?"

Even within the seemingly most unacceptable and painful situation is concealed a deeper good, and within every disaster is contained the seed of grace.

Throughout history, there have been women and men who, in the face of great loss, illness, imprisonment, or impending death, accepted the seemingly unacceptable and thus found "the peace that passeth all understanding."

Acceptance of the unacceptable is the greatest source of grace in this world.

There are situations where all answers and explanations fail. Life does not make sense anymore. Or someone in distress comes to you for help, and you don't know what to do or say.

When you fully accept that you don't know, you give up struggling to find answers with the limited thinking mind, and that is when a greater intelligence can operate through you. And even thought can then benefit from that, since the greater intelligence can flow into it and inspire it.

Sometimes surrender means giving up trying to understand and becoming comfortable with not knowing.

Do you know of someone whose main function in life seems to be to make themselves and others miserable, to spread unhappiness? Forgive them, for they too are part of the awakening of humanity. The role they play represents an intensification of the nightmare of egoic consciousness, the state of non-surrender. There is nothing personal in all this. It is not who they are.

Surrender, one could say, is the inner transition from resistance to acceptance, from "no" to "yes." When you surrender, your sense of self shifts from being identified with a reaction or mental judgment to being the *space around* the reaction or judgment. It is a shift from identification with form — the thought or the emotion — to being and recognizing yourself as that which has no form — spacious awareness.

Whatever you accept completely will take you to peace, including the acceptance that you cannot accept, that you are in resistance.

~

Leave Life alone. Let it be.

~

CHAPTER 7

NATURE

We depend on nature not only for our physical survival. We also need nature to show us the way home, the way out of the prison of our own minds. We got lost in doing, thinking, remembering, anticipating — lost in a maze of complexity and a world of problems.

We have forgotten what rocks, plants, and animals still know. We have forgotten how to *be* — to be still, to be ourselves, to be where life is: Here and Now.

Whenever you bring your attention to anything natural, anything that has come into existence without human intervention, you step out of the prison of conceptualized thinking and, to some extent, participate in the state of connectedness with Being in which everything natural still exists.

To bring your attention to a stone, a tree, or an animal does not mean to *think* about it, but simply to perceive it, to hold it in your awareness.

Something of its essence then transmits itself to you. You can sense how still it is, and in doing so the same stillness arises within you. You sense how deeply it rests in Being — completely at one with what it is and where it is. In realizing this, you too come to a place of rest deep within yourself.

When walking or resting in nature, honor that realm by being there fully. Be still. Look. Listen. See how every animal and every plant is completely itself. Unlike humans, they have not split themselves in two. They do not live through mental images of themselves, so they do not need to be concerned with trying to protect and enhance those images. The deer *is* itself. The daffodil *is* itself.

All things in nature are not only one with themselves but also one with the totality. They haven't removed themselves from the fabric of the whole by claiming a separate existence: "me" and the rest of the universe.

The contemplation of nature can free you of that "me," the great troublemaker.

Bring awareness to the many subtle sounds of nature — the rustling of leaves in the wind, raindrops falling, the humming of an insect, the first birdsong at dawn. Give yourself completely to the act of listening. Beyond the sounds there is something greater: a sacredness that cannot be understood through thought.

You didn't create your body, nor are you able to control the body's functions. An intelligence greater than the human mind is at work. It is the same intelligence that sustains all of nature. You cannot get any closer to that intelligence than by being aware of your own inner energy field — by feeling the aliveness, the animating presence within the body.

The playfulness and joy of a dog, its unconditional love and readiness to celebrate life at any moment often contrast sharply with the inner state of the dog's owner — depressed, anxious, burdened by problems, lost in thought, not present in the only place and only time there is: Here and Now. One wonders: living with this person, how does the dog manage to remain so sane, so joyous?

When you perceive nature only through the mind, through thinking, you cannot sense its aliveness, its beingness. You see the form only and are unaware of the life within the form — the sacred mystery. Thought reduces nature to a commodity to be used in the pursuit of profit or knowledge or some other utilitarian purpose. The ancient forest becomes timber, the bird a research project, the mountain something to be mined or conquered.

When you perceive nature, let there be spaces of no thought, no mind. When you approach nature in this way, it will respond to you and participate in the evolution of human and planetary consciousness.

Notice how present a flower is, how surrendered to life.

The plant that you have in your home — have you ever truly looked at it? Have you allowed that familiar yet mysterious being we call *plant* to teach you its secrets? Have you noticed how deeply peaceful it is? How it is surrounded by a field of stillness? The moment you become aware of a plant's emanation of stillness and peace, that plant becomes your teacher.

Watch an animal, a flower, a tree, and see how it rests in Being. It *is* itself. It has enormous dignity, innocence, and holiness. However, for you to see that, you need to go beyond the mental habit of naming and labeling. The moment you look beyond mental labels, you feel that ineffable dimension of nature that cannot be understood by thought or perceived through the senses. It is a harmony, a sacredness that permeates not only the whole of nature but is also within you.

The air that you breathe is nature, as is the breathing process itself.

Bring your attention to your breathing and realize that you are not doing it. It is the breath of nature. If you had to remember to breathe, you would soon die, and if you tried to stop breathing, nature would prevail.

You reconnect with nature in the most intimate and powerful way by becoming aware of your breathing and learning to hold your attention there. This is a healing and deeply empowering thing to do. It brings about a shift in consciousness from the conceptual world of thought to the inner realm of unconditioned consciousness.

You need nature as your teacher to help you reconnect with Being. But not only do you need nature, it also needs you.

You are not separate from nature. We are all part of the One Life that manifests itself in countless forms throughout the universe, forms that are all completely interconnected. When you recognize the sacredness, the beauty, the incredible stillness and dignity in which a flower or a tree exists, you add something to the flower or the tree. Through your recognition, your awareness, nature too comes to know itself. It comes to know its own beauty and sacredness through you!

A great silent space holds all of nature in its embrace. It also holds you.

Only when you are still inside do you have access to the realm of stillness that rocks, plants, and animals inhabit. Only when your noisy mind subsides can you connect with nature at a deep level and go beyond the sense of separation created by excessive thinking.

Thinking is a stage in the evolution of life. Nature exists in innocent stillness that is prior to the arising of thought. The tree, the flower, the bird, the rock are unaware of their own beauty and sacredness. When human beings become still, they go beyond thought. There is an added dimension of knowing, of awareness, in the stillness that is beyond thought.

Nature can bring you to stillness. That is its gift to you. When you perceive and join with nature in the field of stillness, that field becomes permeated with your awareness. That is your gift to nature.

Through you nature becomes aware of itself. Nature has been waiting for you, as it were, for millions of years.

CHAPTER **8**

RELATIONSHIPS

How quick we are to form an opinion of a person, to come to a conclusion about them. It is satisfying to the egoic mind to label another human being, to give them a conceptual identity, to pronounce righteous judgment upon them.

Every human being has been conditioned to think and behave in certain ways — conditioned genetically as well as by their childhood experiences and their cultural environment.

That is not who they are, but that is who they appear to be. When you pronounce judgment upon someone, you confuse those conditioned mind patterns with who they are. To do that is in itself a deeply conditioned and unconscious pattern. You give them a conceptual identity, and that false identity becomes a prison not only for the other person but also for yourself.

To let go of judgment does not mean that you don't see what they do. It means that you recognize their behavior as a form of conditioning, and you see it and accept it as that. You don't construct an identity out of it for that person.

That liberates you as well as the other person from identification with conditioning, with form, with mind. The ego then no longer runs your relationships.

As long as the ego runs your life, most of your thoughts, emotions, and actions arise from desire and fear. In relationships you then either want or fear something from the other person.

What you want from them may be pleasure or material gain, recognition, praise or attention, or a strengthening of your sense of self through comparison and through establishing that you are, have, or know more than they. What you fear is that the opposite may be the case, and they may diminish your sense of self in some way.

When you make the present moment the focal point of your attention — instead of using it as a means to an end — you go beyond the ego and beyond the unconscious compulsion to use people as a means to an end, the end being self-enhancement at the cost of others. When you give your fullest attention to whoever you are interacting with, you take past and future out of the relationship, except for practical matters. When you are fully present with everyone you meet, you relinquish the conceptual identity you made for them — your interpretation of who they are and what they did in the past — and are able to interact without the egoic movements of desire and fear. Attention, which is alert stillness, is the key.

How wonderful to go beyond wanting and fearing in your relationships. Love does not want or fear anything.

If her past were your past, her pain your pain, her level of consciousness your level of consciousness, you would think and act exactly as she does. With this realization comes forgiveness, compassion, peace.

The ego doesn't like to hear this, because if it cannot be reactive and righteous anymore, it will lose strength.

When you receive whoever comes into the space of Now as a noble guest, when you allow each person to be as they are, they begin to change.

To know another human being in their essence, you don't really need to know anything *about* them — their past, their history, their story. We confuse knowing *about* with a deeper knowing that is non-conceptual. Knowing *about* and knowing are totally different modalities. One is concerned with form, the other with the formless. One operates through thought, the other through stillness.

Knowing *about* is helpful for practical purposes. On that level, we cannot do without it. When it is the predominant modality in relationships, however, it becomes very limiting, even destructive. Thoughts and concepts create an artificial barrier, a separation between human beings. Your interactions are then not rooted in Being, but become mind-based. Without the conceptual barriers, love is naturally present in all human interactions.

Most human interactions are confined to the exchange of words — the realm of thought. It is essential to bring some stillness, particularly into your close relationships.

No relationship can thrive without the sense of spaciousness that comes with stillness. Meditate or spend silent time in nature together. When going for a walk or sitting in the car or at home, become comfortable with being in stillness together. Stillness cannot and need not be created. Just be receptive to the stillness that is already there, but is usually obscured by mental noise.

If spacious stillness is missing, the relationship will be dominated by the mind and can easily be taken over by problems and conflict. If stillness is there, it can contain anything.

True listening is another way of bringing stillness into the relationship. When you truly listen to someone, the dimension of stillness arises and becomes an essential part of the relationship. But true listening is a rare skill. Usually, the greater part of a person's attention is taken up by their thinking. At best, they may be evaluating your words or preparing the next thing to say. Or they may not be listening at all, lost in their own thoughts.

True listening goes far beyond auditory perception. It is the arising of alert attention, a space of presence in which the words are being received. The words now become secondary. They may be meaningful or they may not make sense. Far more important than *what* you are listening to is the act of listening itself, the space of conscious presence that arises as you listen. That space is a unifying field of awareness in which you meet the other person without the separative barriers created by conceptual thinking. And now the other person is no longer "other." In that space, you are joined together as one awareness, one consciousness.

Do you experience frequent and repetitive drama in your close relationships? Do relatively insignificant disagreements often trigger violent arguments and emotional pain?

At the root of such experiences lie the basic egoic patterns: the need to be right and, of course, for someone else to be wrong; that is to say, identification with mental positions. There is also the ego's need to be periodically in conflict with something or someone in order to strengthen its sense of separation between "me" and the "other" without which it cannot survive.

In addition, there is the accumulated emotional pain from the past that you and each human being carries within, both from your personal past as well as the collective pain of humanity that goes back a long, long time. This "pain-body" is an energy field within you that sporadically takes you over because it needs to experience more emotional pain for it to feed on and replenish itself. It will try to control your thinking and make it deeply negative. It loves your negative thoughts, since it resonates with their frequency and so can feed on them. It will also provoke negative emotional reactions in people close to you, especially your partner, in order to feed on the ensuing drama and emotional pain.

How can you free yourself from this deep-seated unconscious identification with pain that creates so much misery in your life?

Become aware of it. Realize that it is not who you are, and recognize it for what it is: past pain. Witness it as it happens in your partner or in yourself. When your unconscious identification with it is broken, when you are able to observe it within yourself, you don't feed it anymore, and it will gradually lose its energy charge.

Human interaction can be hell. Or it can be a great spiritual practice.

When you look upon another human being and feel great love toward them, or when you contemplate beauty in nature and something within you responds deeply to it, close your eyes for a moment and feel the essence of that love or that beauty within you, inseparable from who you are, your true nature. The outer form is a temporary reflection of what you are within, in your essence. That is why love and beauty can never leave you, although all outer forms will.

What is your relationship with the world of objects, the countless things that surround you and that you handle every day? The chair you sit on, the pen, the car, the cup? Are they to you merely a means to an end, or do you occasionally acknowledge their existence, their being, no matter how briefly, by noticing them and giving them your attention?

When you get attached to objects, when you are using them to enhance your worth in your own eyes and in the eyes of others, concern about things can easily take over your whole life. When there is self-identification with things, you don't appreciate them for what they are because you are looking for yourself in them.

When you appreciate an object for what it is, when you acknowledge its being without mental projection, you cannot *not* feel grateful for its existence. You may also sense that it is not really inanimate, that it only appears so to the senses. Physicists will confirm that on a molecular level it is indeed a pulsating energy field.

Through selfless appreciation of the realm of things, the world around you will come alive in ways that you cannot even begin to comprehend with the mind.

Whenever you meet anyone, no matter how briefly, do you acknowledge their being by giving them your full attention? Or are you reducing them to a means to an end, a mere function or role?

What is the quality of your relationship with the cashier at the supermarket, the parking attendant, the repairman, the "customer"?

A moment of attention is enough. As you look at them or listen to them, there is an alert stillness — perhaps only two or three seconds, perhaps longer. That is enough for something more real to emerge than the roles we usually play and identify with. All roles are part of the conditioned consciousness that is the human mind. That which emerges through the act of attention is the unconditioned — who you are in your essence, underneath your name and form. You are no longer acting out a script; you become real. When that dimension emerges from within you, it also draws it forth from within the other person.

Ultimately, of course, there is no other, and you are always meeting yourself.

~

CHAPTER 9

DEATH & THE ETERNAL

When you walk through a forest that has not been tamed and interfered with by man, you will see not only abundant life all around you, but you will also encounter fallen trees and decaying trunks, rotting leaves and decomposing matter at every step. Wherever you look, you will find death as well as life.

Upon closer scrutiny, however, you will discover that the decomposing tree trunk and rotting leaves not only give birth to new life, but are full of life themselves. Microorganisms are at work. Molecules are rearranging themselves. So death isn't to be found anywhere. There is only the metamorphosis of life forms. What can you learn from this?

Death is not the opposite of life. Life has no opposite. The opposite of death is birth. Life is eternal.

Sages and poets throughout the ages have recognized the dreamlike quality of human existence — seemingly so solid and real and yet so fleeting that it could dissolve at any moment.

At the hour of your death, the story of your life may, indeed, appear to you like a dream that is coming to an end. Yet even in a dream there must be an essence that is real. There must be a consciousness in which the dream happens; otherwise, it would not be.

That consciousness — does the body create it or does consciousness create the dream of body, the dream of somebody?

Why have most of those who went through a near-death experience lost their fear of death? Reflect upon this.

Of course you know you are going to die, but that remains a mere mental concept until you meet death "in person" for the first time: through a serious illness or an accident that happens to you or someone close to you, or through the passing away of a loved one, death enters your life as the awareness of your own mortality.

Most people turn away from it in fear, but if you do not flinch and face the fact that your body is fleeting and could dissolve at any moment, there is some degree of disidentification, however slight, from your own physical and psychological form, the "me." When you see and accept the impermanent nature of all life forms, a strange sense of peace comes upon you.

Through facing death, your consciousness is freed to some extent from identification with form. This is why in some Buddhist traditions, the monks regularly visit the morgue to sit and meditate among the dead bodies.

There is still a widespread denial of death in Western cultures. Even old people try not to speak or think about it, and dead bodies are hidden away. A culture that denies death inevitably becomes shallow and superficial, concerned only with the external form of things. When death is denied, life loses its depth. The possibility of knowing who we are beyond name and form, the dimension of the transcendent, disappears from our lives because death is the opening into that dimension.

People tend to be uncomfortable with endings, because every ending is a little death. That's why in many languages, the word for "good-bye" means "see you again."

Whenever an experience comes to an end — a gathering of friends, a vacation, your children leaving home — you die a little death. A "form" that appeared in your consciousness as that experience dissolves. Often this leaves behind a feeling of emptiness that most people try hard not to feel, not to face.

If you can learn to accept and even welcome the endings in your life, you may find that the feeling of emptiness that initially felt uncomfortable turns into a sense of inner spaciousness that is deeply peaceful.

By learning to die daily in this way, you open yourself to Life.

Most people feel that their identity, their sense of self, is something incredibly precious that they don't want to lose. That is why they have such fear of death.

It seems unimaginable and frightening that "I" could cease to exist. But you confuse that precious "I" with your name and form and a story associated with it. That "I" is no more than a temporary formation in the field of consciousness.

As long as that form identity is all you know, you are not aware that this preciousness is your own essence, your innermost sense of *I Am,* which is consciousness itself. It is the eternal in you — and that's the only thing you *cannot* lose.

Whenever any kind of deep loss occurs in your life — such as loss of possessions, your home, a close relationship; or loss of your reputation, job, or physical abilities — something inside you dies. You feel diminished in your sense of who you are. There may also be a certain disorientation. "Without this...who am I?"

When a form that you had unconsciously identified with as part of yourself leaves you or dissolves, that can be extremely painful. It leaves a hole, so to speak, in the fabric of your existence.

When this happens, don't deny or ignore the pain or the sadness that you feel. Accept that it is there. Beware of your mind's tendency to construct a story around that loss in which you are assigned the role of victim. Fear, anger, resentment, or self-pity are the emotions that go with that role. Then become aware of what lies behind those emotions as well as behind the mind-made story: that hole, that empty space. Can you face and accept that strange sense of emptiness? If you do, you may find that it is no longer a fearful place. You may be surprised to find peace emanating from it.

Whenever death occurs, whenever a life form dissolves, God, the formless and unmanifested, shines through the opening left by the dissolving form. That is why the most sacred thing in life is death. That is why the peace of God can come to you through the contemplation and acceptance of death.

How short-lived every human experience is, how fleeting our lives. Is there anything that is not subject to birth and death, anything that is eternal?

Consider this: if there were only one color, let us say blue, and the entire world and everything in it were blue, then there would be no blue. There needs to be something that is not blue so that blue can be recognized; otherwise, it would not "stand out," would not exist.

In the same way, does it not require something that is not fleeting and impermanent for the fleetingness of all things to be recognized? In other words: if everything, including yourself, were impermanent, would you even know it? Does the fact that you are aware of and can witness the short-lived nature of all forms, including your own, not mean that there is something in you that is not subject to decay?

When you are twenty, you are aware of your body as strong and vigorous; sixty years later, you are aware of your body as weakened and old. Your thinking too may have changed from when you were twenty, but the awareness that knows that your body is young or old or that your thinking has changed has undergone no change. That awareness is the eternal in you — consciousness itself. It is the formless One Life. Can you lose It? No, because you are It.

Some people become deeply peaceful and almost luminous just before they die, as if something is shining through the dissolving form.

Sometimes it happens that very ill or old people become almost transparent, so to speak, in the last few weeks, months, or even years of their lives. As they look at you, you may see a light shining through their eyes. There is no psychological suffering left. They have surrendered and so the person, the mind-made egoic "me," has already dissolved. They have "died before they died" and found the deep inner peace that is the realization of the deathless within themselves.

To every accident and disaster there is a potentially redemptive dimension that we are usually unaware of.

The tremendous shock of totally unexpected, imminent death can have the effect of forcing your consciousness completely out of identification with form. In the last few moments before physical death, and as you die, you then experience yourself as consciousness free of form. Suddenly, there is no more fear, just peace and a knowing that "all is well" and that death is only a form dissolving. Death is then recognized as ultimately illusory — as illusory as the form you had identified with as yourself.

Death is not an anomaly or the most dreadful of all events as modern culture would have you believe, but the most natural thing in the world, inseparable from and just as natural as its polarity — birth. Remind yourself of this when you sit with a dying person.

It is a great privilege and a sacred act to be present at a person's death as a witness and companion.

When you sit with a dying person, do not deny any aspect of that experience. Do not deny what is happening and do not deny your feelings. The recognition that there is nothing you can do may make you feel helpless, sad, or angry. Accept what you feel. Then go one step further: accept that there is nothing you can do, and accept it completely. You are not in control. Deeply surrender to every aspect of that experience, your feelings as well as any pain or discomfort the dying person may be experiencing. Your surrendered state of consciousness and the stillness that comes with it will greatly assist the dying person and ease their transition. If words are called for, they will come out of the stillness within you. But they will be secondary.

With the stillness comes the benediction: peace.

CHAPTER 10

SUFFERING &
THE END OF SUFFERING

The interconnectedness of all things: Buddhists have always known it, and physicists now confirm it. Nothing that happens is an isolated event; it only appears to be. The more we judge and label it, the more we isolate it. The wholeness of life becomes fragmented through our thinking. Yet the totality of life has brought this event about. It is part of the web of interconnectedness that is the cosmos.

This means: whatever *is* could not be otherwise.

In most cases, we cannot begin to understand what role a seemingly senseless event may have within the totality of the cosmos, but recognizing its inevitability within the vastness of the whole can be the beginning of an inner acceptance of what *is* and thus a realignment with the wholeness of life.

True freedom and the end of suffering is living in such a way as if you had completely chosen whatever you feel or experience at this moment.

This inner alignment with Now is the end of suffering.

Is suffering really necessary? Yes and no.

If you had not suffered as you have, there would be no depth to you as a human being, no humility, no compassion. You would not be reading this now. Suffering cracks open the shell of ego, and then comes a point when it has served its purpose. Suffering is necessary until you realize it is unnecessary.

Unhappiness needs a mind-made "me" with a story, a conceptual identity. It needs time — past and future. When you remove time from your unhappiness, what is it that remains? The "such-ness" of this moment remains.

It may be a feeling of heaviness, agitation, tightness, anger, or even nausea. That is not unhappiness, and it is not a personal problem. There is nothing personal in human pain. It is simply an intense pressure or intense energy that you feel some-where in the body. By giving it attention, the feel-ing doesn't turn into thinking and thus reactivate the unhappy "me."

See what happens when you just allow a feeling to be.

Much suffering, much unhappiness arises when you take each thought that comes into your head for the truth. Situations don't make you unhappy. They may cause you physical pain, but they don't make you unhappy. Your thoughts make you unhappy. Your interpretations, the stories you tell yourself make you unhappy.

"The thoughts I am thinking right now are making me unhappy." This realization breaks your unconscious identification with those thoughts.

What a miserable day.

He didn't have the decency to return my call.

She let me down.

Little stories we tell ourselves and others, often in the form of complaints. They are unconsciously designed to enhance our always deficient sense of self through being "right" and making something or someone "wrong." Being "right" places us in a position of imagined superiority and so strengthens our false sense of self, the ego. This also creates some kind of enemy: yes, the ego needs enemies to define its boundary, and even the weather can serve that function.

Through habitual mental judgment and emotional contraction, you have a personalized, reactive relationship to people and events in your life. These are all forms of self-created suffering, but they are not recognized as such because to the ego they are satisfying. The ego enhances itself through reactivity and conflict.

How simple life would be without those stories.

It is raining.

He did not call.

I was there. She was not.

When you are suffering, when you are unhappy, stay totally with what is Now. Unhappiness or problems cannot survive in the Now.

Suffering begins when you mentally name or label a situation in some way as undesirable or bad. You resent a situation and that resentment personalizes it and brings in a reactive "me."

Naming and labeling are habitual, but that habit can be broken. Start practicing "not naming" with small things. If you miss the plane, drop and break a cup, or slip and fall in the mud, can you refrain from naming the experience as bad or painful? Can you immediately accept the "isness" of that moment?

Naming something as bad causes an emotional contraction within you. When you let it be, without naming it, enormous power is suddenly available to you.

The contraction cuts you off from that power, the power of life itself.

They ate the fruit of the tree of the knowledge of good and evil.

Go beyond good and bad by refraining from mentally labeling anything as good or bad. When you go beyond the habitual naming, the power of the universe moves through you. When you are in a nonreactive relationship to experiences, what you would have called "bad" before often turns around quickly, if not immediately, through the power of life itself.

Watch what happens when you don't name an experience as "bad" and instead bring an inner acceptance, an inner "yes" to it, and so let it be as it is.

Whatever your life situation is, how would you feel if you completely accepted it as it is — right Now?

There are many subtle and not so subtle forms of suffering that are so "normal" they are usually not recognized as suffering and may even feel satisfying to the ego — irritation, impatience, anger, having an issue with something or someone, resentment, complaining.

You can learn to recognize all those forms of suffering as they happen and know: at this moment, I am creating suffering for myself.

If you are in the habit of creating suffering for yourself, you are probably creating suffering for others too. These unconscious mind patterns tend to come to an end simply by making them conscious, by becoming aware of them as they happen.

You cannot be conscious *and* create suffering for yourself.

This is the miracle: behind every condition, person, or situation that appears "bad" or "evil" lies concealed a deeper good. That deeper good reveals itself to you — both within and without — through inner acceptance of what *is*.

"Resist not evil" is one of the highest truths of humanity.

A dialogue:

Accept what is.

I truly cannot. I'm agitated and angry about this.

Then accept what is.

Accept that I'm agitated and angry? Accept that I cannot accept?

Yes. Bring acceptance into your nonacceptance. Bring surrender into your nonsurrender. Then see what happens.

Chronic physical pain is one of the harshest teachers you can have. "Resistance is futile" is its teaching.

Nothing could be more normal than an unwillingness to suffer. Yet if you can let go of that unwillingness, and instead allow the pain to be there, you may notice a subtle inner separation from the pain, a space between you and the pain, as it were. This means to suffer consciously, willingly. When you suffer consciously, physical pain can quickly burn up the ego in you, since ego consists largely of resistance. The same is true of extreme physical disability.

You "offer up your suffering to God" is another way of saying this.

You don't need to be a Christian to understand the deep universal truth that is contained in symbolic form in the image of the cross.

The cross is a torture instrument. It stands for the most extreme suffering, limitation, and helplessness a human being can encounter. Then suddenly that human being surrenders, suffers willingly, consciously, expressed through the words, "Not my will but Thy will be done." At that moment, the cross, the torture instrument, shows its hidden face: it is also a sacred symbol, a symbol for the divine.

That which seemed to deny the existence of any transcendental dimension to life, through surrender becomes an opening into that dimension.

ABOUT THE AUTHOR

Eckhart Tolle was born in Germany, where he spent the first thirteen years of his life. After graduating from the University of London, he was a research scholar and supervisor at Cambridge University. When he was twenty-nine, a profound spiritual transformation virtually dissolved his old identity and radically changed the course of his life.

The next few years were devoted to understanding, integrating, and deepening that transformation, which marked the beginning of an intense inward journey.

Eckhart is not aligned with any particular religion or tradition. In his teaching, he conveys a simple yet profound message with the timeless and uncomplicated clarity of the ancient spiritual masters: there is a way out of suffering and into peace.

Eckhart is currently traveling extensively, taking his teachings and his presence throughout the world. He has lived in Vancouver, Canada, since 1996.

For information on talks, satsangs, intensives,
retreats, and meditations given by Eckhart Tolle see:

www.eckharttolle.com

For further details, contact:
Yogi Impressions LLP
1711, Centre 1, World Trade Centre,
Cuffe Parade, Mumbai 400 005, India.

Fill in the Mailing List form on our website
and receive, via email, information on
books, authors, events and more.
Visit: www.yogiimpressions.com

Telephone: (022) 61541500, 61541541
E-mail: yogi@yogiimpressions.com

 Join us on Facebook:
www.facebook.com/yogiimpressions

The Sacred India Tarot
Inspired by Indian Mythology and Epics
78 cards + 4 bonus cards + 350 page handbook
The Sacred India Tarot is truly an offering from India to the world.
It is the first and only Tarot deck that works solely within the
parameters of sacred Indian mythology – almost the world's only
living mythology today.

DVDs

AUDIO CDs

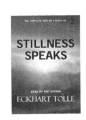